Collected Poems

by Patricia Pickworth

Copyright Patricia Pickworth
All rights reserved

Published by United Press Ltd
2002

A CIP catalogue record for this book is available from the British Library.

ISBN 1-904169-03-1

© Copyright Patricia Pickworth 2002

CLASSIFICATION: POETRY

This book is sold under the condition that it shall not, by way of trade or otherwise, be lent, resold, hired out or otherwise circulated without the publisher's prior consent in any form of binding or cover other than that in which it is published and without a similar condition including this condition being imposed on the subsequent purchaser.

Printed and bound in Great Britain.
First published in Great Britain in 2002 by
United Press Ltd
44A St James Street
Burnley
BB11 1NQ
Tel: 01282 459533
Fax: 01282 412679
All Rights Reserved

www.upltd.co.uk

ARTHUR PICKWORTH 1920 - 2001

We made our Golden Wedding,
I didn't think we would
You'd been so very ill, my dear,
It didn't look too good

But with our children round us
We had a pleasant time
I thought I'd like to remember it
With this little rhyme.

CONTENTS

5	Seasons
	Sonnet
6	Skylark
7	Minka
	Learning Curve
8	To Buck - In Memorian RAF - 1941
	The Soldier. Belgium 1940
9	Reflection
10	Melody
11	South Downs in Winter
	Symphony No 5
12	England - Elegy
	Tranquility
13	Chanctonbury Ring
14	St James, Piccadilly 1940
	Aftermath - December 1945
15	To Those Who fell in Burma
	Father
16	Alive
	Stroke

4

SEASONS

In January a cosy firelit room
In February the early Snowdrops bloom
In March the yellow Crocuses appear
In April Primroses and purple Violets dear
In May the dainty Cherry blossoms blow
In June the scarlet Rose sways to and frow
In July the Pansies faces smile
In August Gladioli bloom awhile
In September Apples ripen on the tree
In October Chestnuts fall for you and me
In November the leaves begin to fall
In December Holly for the Christmas Hall

SONNET

The wooded hills are golden with the light
That shines from out the Sun so radiant bright
The shadows play upon the sunlit hill
The stream flows on beside the ruined mill
The Primrose grows upon the Moss beside
And Violets 'neath their tiny leaves do hide
The Swallows dip and play about the stream
While I lie on my back and idly dream

SKYLARK

A lovely Poem is a thing
That lasts and does not fade
Some people though, think any Joy
Or beauty is not made, to last
But beauty never dies

The Glory of the Skylark song
Which soon doth melt away
Leaves us feeling sadly
That all beauties die one day
Should a poet inspired by birds
Write thus of Him in Glorying words.
Oh Love! What beauty have we fast
These words enchantment give.
The song which with the fading light
Falls on the air, may live Eternally
For one who hears the Exquisite sound
That brings forth tears
Why say they then that every joy
Which we perchance embrace
Should leave a grieving soul behind
Before we end our race.
For if this joy expressed can be
Upon a scroll. It's lasting beauty see.

MINKA

How like a soft grey mist you seem to be
Whose fur has all the softness of the dawn
And yet your eyes, so like the night, can see
When all the world is waiting for the morn
What thoughts lie in that dainty head
What certain death beneath those padded paws
What mask of Sphinx like silence as though dead
Like old Egyptian Idols; For their laws
Proclaimed the glory of your endless race
That they might idolise some living thing
So like themselves in sleek and silent grace
Immortal now beyond all doubt, you bring
To us a sense of Dignity and Grace
Within our lives, and fill an envied place.

LEARNING CURVE

Some day perhaps my heart will glean
Those precious thoughts and all that they might mean
Those treasures hid within the depths of words
In babbling brooklets and the singing birds
In nature and in books the truth is told
No truer Champion, no finer mould
Of beauty, knowledge or of duty stern
Of all the mysteries I seek to learn
So much there is in life I strive to know
From humblest understanding to the glow
Of higher thoughts, beneath whose sphere I move
The smallest word may yet a harvest prove
Before my numbered days draw to a close
Perchance I'll find a balm for worldly woes

TO BUCK - IN MEMORIAN RAF - 1941

How sad this life should so be strewn away
Before the light of youth had spent its day
So young - His heart still trembled with the joys
Of well remembered pleasures; so destroys
With rapid terror, fates sad destiny
Life, love and beauty can no more sue,
So fair and generous he, and yet they drew
Him from his dearly treasured life - and
Part of God's pure earth and this fair land
Claimed him for her own grim sacrifice
Upon her verdant altar: This device
so cunning made by man's own hand
Sadly commingled with the trees into another land

THE SOLDIER. BELGIUM 1940

A Soldier dies; We know just this of him
That he in duty to his country died
The battle cry his only burial hymn
His rifle and his helmet at his side
Englands pride and freedom were his aim
And to this purpose gave his simple life
Honoured by all, though no one knew his name
He played his part to end the reign of strife
The whole world mourns and with a solemn sigh
Bequeaths him to his lonely foreign grave
Far beyond England's soil. Gods blue sky
Watches unceasing o'er the unknown brave
Who lie in silent protest 'gainst the laws
That drive sane men into ungodly wars

REFLECTION

A fleeting year ago we two were laughing
Laughing at life and all it held in store
We little knew what sudden blinding vision
Would rob us of our carefree joys. No more
To roam the sombre hills and shadowed lanes
No more our footprints skim the red grained sand
Our eyes behold the sea as sunset wanes,
No more in summer's brazen heat to lie
Beneath the gnarled green oak our senses fill
With soft brown moss-earth smelling; golden leaves
The glory of last year's prime, still
Pillow on their breasts Springs mortal children
What right have we to grieve that he is gone
His short part played; a new life dearly won.

MELODY

What simple beauty now divides my soul
In these tormented agonies of sound
How like and yet unlike thy hallowed voice
These single, solemn notes float heaven - bound.
As they ascend they waver in the trees
And whisper notes of solemn melody
Like to the gentle murmuring of the breeze
Sensuously swaying the verdant leaves
And like the liquid fire of purest song
That from the Skylark's suppliant throat
Pours in volume divinely soft yet strong
To reach It's goal - the infinite blue sky
The ceiling of the universe - to fade and die.

SOUTH DOWNS IN WINTER

The hills in sullen beauty stand
The clouds go racing by
The sylvan rustle of the crazéd leaves
The changing glory of the sky.
All these my mazéd eyes enthral
Thro' winter's soft and sudden moods
I hear the intruding cuckoo's sad ghost call
O'er the damp stillness of the solemn woods
Behind their misty curtain peep
The grey green drifting, rainswept downs
Shyly they peer and then draw back once more
Hiding away from Winters harsh stern frowns
The soft wool clouds majestic pass
Across the heaving wintry sky
Swirling and dancing with such carefree joy
Mine be their happy lot I cry.

SYMPHONY NO 5

To night I have been borne on dulcet wings
High above the world and all it's sordid ways
I have felt the kiss of silver cloudlets
And seen the smile of fleeting stars
I have heard the burst of a million songs
Cascading crystal sounds about my ears
drunk with music; my soul, free as the wind
Soaring high in moonlit infinity.

ENGLAND - ELEGY

Mother with unbowed head
Hear then across the sea
The farewell of the dead
The dead who died for thee.
Greet them again with tender words
Saving thee, they could not save themselves

TRANQUILITY

The soft insistent singing of the birds
Skylarks hidden in the infinite sky
Soothe my sad heart, the gentle whispering breeze
Cools my hot brow, that I may quietly lie
And solve my problems and the worlds!

CHANCTONBURY RING

Sussex, thy hills indeed are nobly crowned
With rings of purest Autumn gold and brown
That fading sunset's rosy sky has drowned
In floods of fiery red from Heaven hurled down.
When twilight's hues fade slowly into mist
Thy crown becomes a lonely sentinel
By all the winds in Heaven gently kissed
Wooed by the sky whose ways it knows so well
Noblest of Crowns is Chanctonbury Ring
Beneath whose spell lies dreaming Wiston Lake
Reflecting the evening sky with glorious gold
Shaking her hair to make the ripples wake.
The beauty of these Downs brings joy and peace
And from the weary daily toil - release!

ST JAMES CHURCH, PICCADILLY 1940

The blackened rafters claw the granite sky
In dumb appealing that their woes be heard
They did not ask that they should be so maimed
For maimed they are! Their blood no longer stirred
To fiery rapture by sweet hymns of praise
But scorched and blackened by the flames of hell
Let loose upon the earth, oh futile days to come
Of war and death! And blacker days as well
Of bitter reconstruction; turn not back
To those gay shadows of our pre - war souls.
Our shattered buildings can no more return
To former beauty; rent with gaping holes
They stand; a symbol warning us - beware!
We have so much to win, to lose, to dare.

AFTERMATH - DECEMBER 1945

With thoughts of Peace and Joy, Soul quietening streams
God's pleasant truths shine down into my heart
And pierce right through my mind's conflicting dreams
That help me find the only way to start
Unravelling the tangled thoughts of war
Which prance and charge unbidden in my brain.
Somewhere beneath all battered and unsure
My thoughts of times long past emerge again
And shake their bruiséd heads and slowly smile
The world they thought was dead must surely be
Re-born, re-schooled and brought once more to trial
By those who fought to make this mad world free
What of the verdict? Can we make it sure
This peace of ours and turn our backs on war.

TO THOSE WHO FELL IN BURMA

They fell together - Poet, Miner, Clerk
What can we show them for their sacrifice?
They walked with upheld heads into the dark
Still nothingness of death, how high the price
For which they thought to buy our children peace!
What have we done to prove their simple worth?
They were but men - they loved as we - and yet
For these their homes - no matter what their birth
They bore the strangeness of this alien land
With humour to the last. The jungle called
And they - for our tomorrow - took her hand
Her strong green arms embraced them, they enthralled
Gave their today that we might live anew
Not only for ourselves but for them too!

FATHER

Within the house there is an empty space
The absence of a well loved face
The stillness of a voice that is not heard
Not e'er a look, a smile, nor yet a word
Only the joy of happiness that's past
Can ease the darkness of the mind o'ercast
Only the memory of bygone years
Can stem the gentle flood of tears
No other one can ever quite replace
The fast held memory of your loving face
No one, tho' they are loved can be the same
As you dear mentor who gave me your name

ALIVE

When your eyes start getting dimmer
And your life begins to simmer off the boil!
You're not getting any slimmer
And you rather think a zimmer's getting near!
Your back complains each time you bend
All you can do is try and mend -
With massage oil!
You get a pain and heaven forfend
Is this the beginning of the end? never fear
Thanks to the Lord above
And all those near you love,
And who love you, you're alive!

STROKE

When we see you lying there
What thoughts are going through your head?
Thoughts and feelings you can't express
Because that piece of brain is dead
Three whole years of silent pain
Unable to return our loving chatter
If only you could speak again!
Even to grumble! It wouldn't matter
We love you dearly but are not sure
If we can bear to watch and wait
Until at last you are set free
From your intolerable state.
Give us the strength to go on apace
And still show you a loving face.